Preparing for KREUTZER

(Published in Two Volumes)

An Intermediate Course of Violin Study

Based on the Famous Works of Kayser, Mazas,

Dont, De Beriot, Dancla, Blumenstengel, and

Other Masters of the Violin Repertoire

by HARVEY S. WHISTLER

RUBANK®

HAL•LEONARD®
CORPORATION
7777 W. BLUEMOUND RD. P.O. BOX 13819 MILWAUKEE, WI 53213

For DAILY PRACTICE and for REVIEW

COMPREHENSIVE COURSE OF STUDY

Developing Bowing

WHISTLER

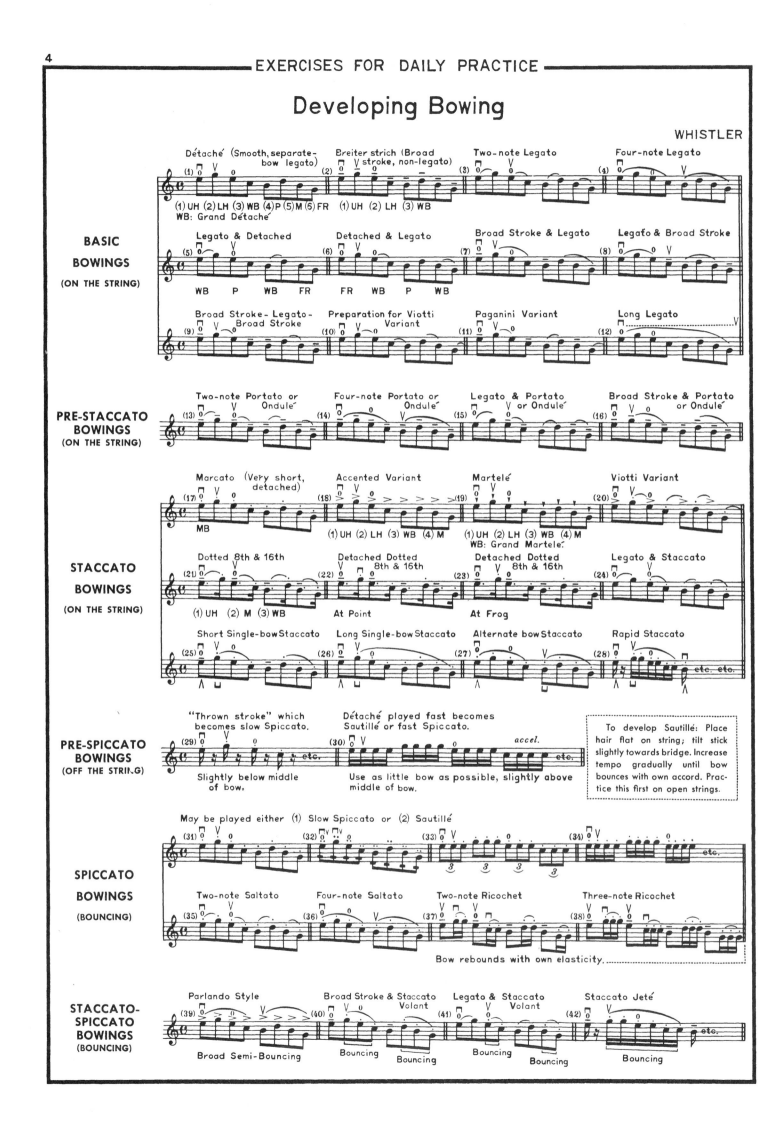

Etude for Developing Bowing

KAYSER, Op. 20

To be memorized. All bowing variants of opposite page should be systematically applied to this etude.

* $\widehat{4}$: Extend fourth finger while hand remains in same position.

Developing Finger Strength

EICHBERG
from the
METHOD FOR VIOLIN

◇ = Fingers to be held down but not active in producing tones.

Practice slowly. Raise fingers in a deliberate manner. Listen carefully to intonation. Repeat each exercise several times.

Also practice (1) slurring each four notes, and (2) slurring each eight notes.

Developing Intonation

SCHRADIECK
from the
TECHNICAL VIOLIN SCHOOL

Also practice very slowly, using a separate bow for each tone. Repeat each line several times.

* $\widehat{4}$ = Fourth finger extended.

Etudes In First Position

Etude in G

WEISS, Op. 80

To be played with broad strokes of the bow.

Also practice using (1) détaché bowings, as well as other basic variants, (2) selected staccato variants, and (3) selected spiccato variants.

Etude in D

KAYSER, Op. 20

To be played in legato style.

Also practice with a separate bow for each note, using (1) détaché bowings, as well as other basic variants, (2) selected staccato variants, and (3) selected spiccato variants.

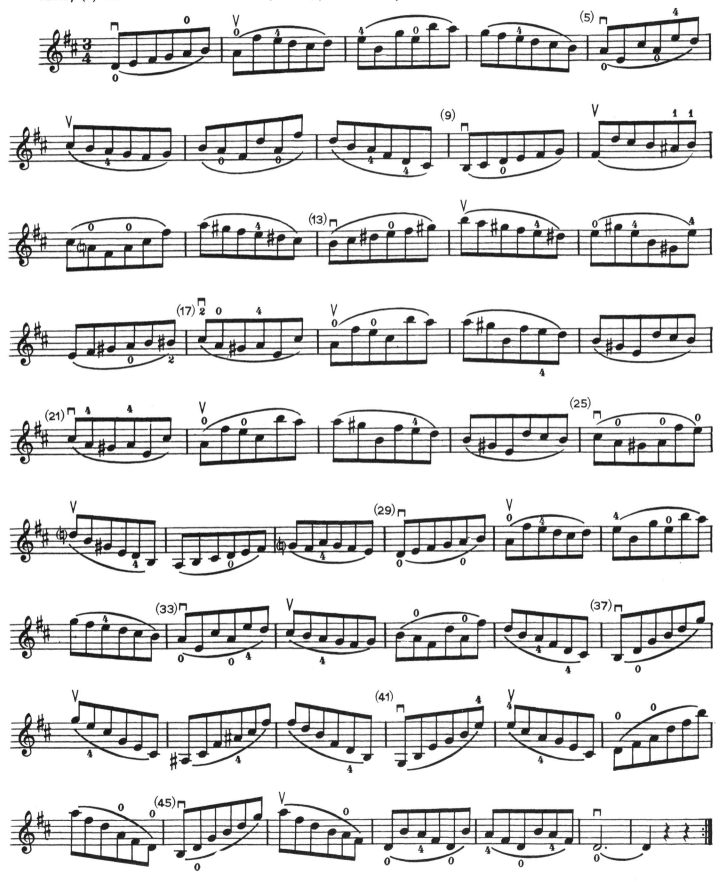

Etude in F

KAYSER, Op. 20

Maintain a firm, steady bow throughout. Observe proper bow division at all times.

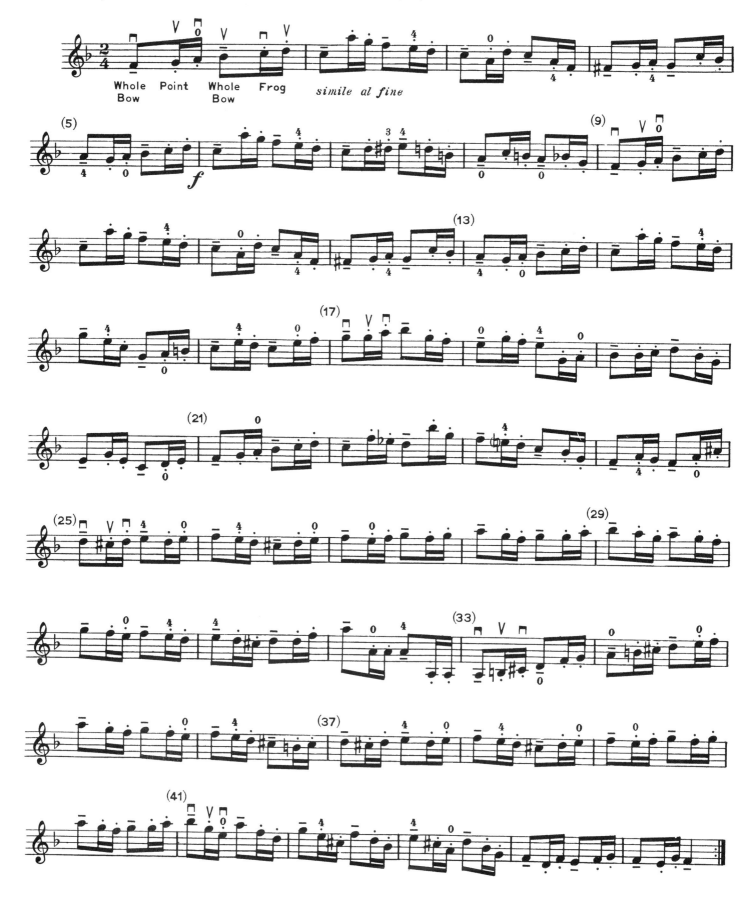

Etude in B♭

KAYSER, Op. 20

To be played in martelé style.

Also practice using (1) détaché bowings, as well as other basic variants, (2) selected staccato variants, and (3) selected spiccato variants.

Etude in A

KAYSER, Op. 20

To be played with broad strokes of the bow.

Also practice using (1) détaché bowings, as well as other basic variants, (2) selected staccato variants, and (3) selected spiccato variants.

Etude in E

WOHLFAHRT, Op. 54

To be played with spiccato bowing, using selected variants of same.

Also practice using (1) détaché bowings, as well as other basic variants, and (2) selected staccato variants.

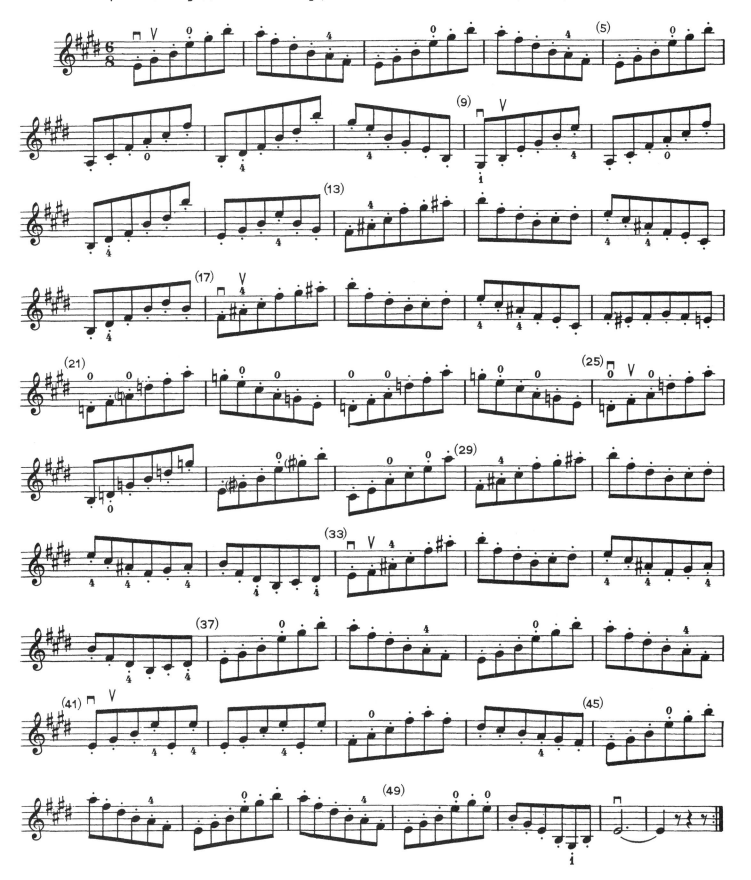

Etude in E♭

DE BERIOT, Op. 102

To be played in legato style.

Also practice slurring only four notes in each bow.

Also practice using (1) détaché bowings, as well as other basic variants, (2) selected staccato variants, and (3) selected spiccato variants.

Etude in A♭

SPOHR
from the
VIOLIN SCHOOL

To be played in legato style. Maintain a smooth, steady tempo throughout.

Position Playing

> If difficulty is encountered in playing the studies on this page, the performer should turn at once to INTRODUCING THE POSITIONS, Vols. 1 & 2, by Harvey S. Whistler, and begin a more thorough review of the higher positions.

DE BERIOT, Op. 102

SECOND POSITION

THIRD POSITION

FOURTH POSITION

FIFTH POSITION

SIXTH POSITION

SEVENTH POSITION

Etudes In Higher Positions

Etude in C

DANCLA, Op. 52

To be played entirely in SECOND POSITION, using broad strokes of the bow.

Also practice using (1) détaché bowings, as well as other basic variants, (2) selected staccato variants, and (3) selected spiccato variants.

Etude No. 1 in G

MAZAS, Op. 36

To be played with broad strokes of the bow.

Also practice using (1) détaché bowings, as well as other basic variants, (2) selected staccato variants, and (3) selected spiccato variants.

Etude No. 2 in G

DONT, Op. 37

To be played in legato style.

Also practice using but one bow for each complete measure. Maintain a smooth, steady tempo throughout.

Etude No. 1 in D

KAYSER, Op. 20

To be played with spiccato bowing, using selected variants of the same.

Also practice using (1) détaché bowings, as well as other basic variants, and (2) selected staccato variants.

* $\underbrace{1}$ = Draw back first finger while hand remains in same position.

Etude No. 2 in D

MAZAS, Op. 36

To be played with broad strokes of the bow.

Also practice using (1) détaché bowings, as well as other basic variants, (2) selected staccato variants, and (3) selected spiccato variants.

Etude No. 1 in F

BLUMENSTENGEL, Op. 33

To be played in a firm, forceful manner.

Also practice using selected spiccato variants.

Etude No. 2 in F

DONT, Op. 37

To be·played in a firm, forceful manner.

Also practice using selected spiccato variants.

Etude No. 1 in B♭

MAZAS, Op. 36

To be played in martelé style.

Also practice using (1) détaché bowings, as well as other basic variants, (2) selected staccato variants, and (3) selected spiccato variants.

Etude No. 2 in B♭

MAZAS, Op. 36

To be played in legato style. Maintain a smooth, steady tempo throughout. All shifting should be inaudible.

Etude No. 1 in A

DONT, Op. 37

To be played in legato style. Maintain a smooth, steady tempo throughout.

Etude No. 2 in A

WEISS, Op. 80

To be played in a smooth, flowing style, with a light accent on each principal note following an embellishment.

Etude No. 1 in E♭

SPOHR
from the
VIOLIN SCHOOL

To be played in legato style. The withdrawal of the fourth finger from the extension should be accomplished, in each instance, with as much smoothness as possible, using a rapid, light portamento movement.

Etude No. 2 in E♭

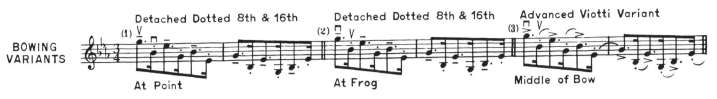

BOWING VARIANTS

Detached Dotted 8th & 16th — At Point
Detached Dotted 8th & 16th — At Frog
Advanced Viotti Variant — Middle of Bow

KAYSER, Op. 20

The dotted eighth note should be broad in effect, and the sixteenth note that follows, short and abrupt.

Etude No. 1 in E

MAZAS, Op. 36

Practice slowly at first. Septuplets should be grouped as indicated by brackets (▯▯▯▯ ▯▯▯). Maintain a steady tempo throughout; do not retard speed on septuplet groupings.

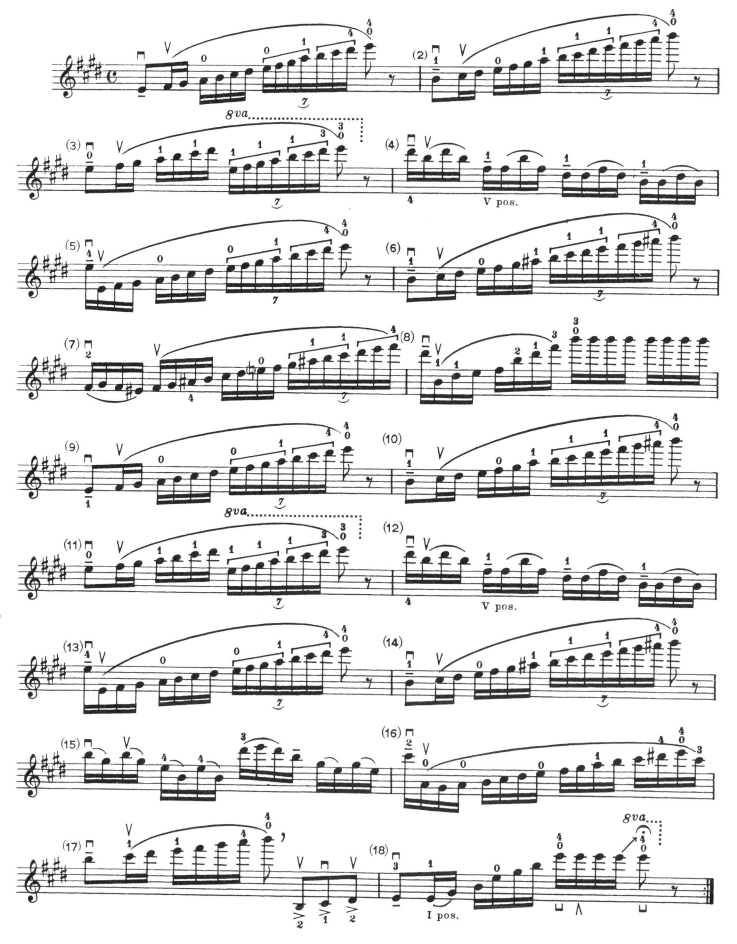

Etude No. 2 in E

BOWING VARIANTS

SPOHR
from the
VIOLIN SCHOOL

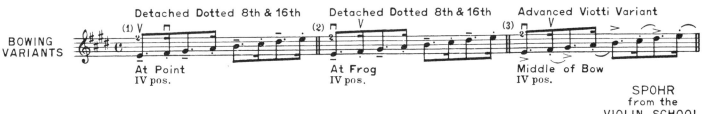

To be played entirely in FOURTH POSITION. The dotted eighth note should be broad in effect, and the sixteenth note that follows, short and abrupt.

(Remain in FOURTH POSITION throughout.)

Etude No. 1 in A♭

KAYSER, Op. 20

Shifting of positions should be inaudible throughout.

Also practice with a separate bow for each note, using (1) selected staccato variants, and (2) selected spiccato variants.

Etude No. 2 in A♭

SITT, Op. 32

To be played entirely in FOURTH POSITION. The tone should commence distinctly and remain free and un-
hampered throughout.

Developing Finger Velocity

Also practice each exercise using (1) a separate bow for each note, (2) slurring FOUR notes in each bow, and (3) slurring EIGHT notes in each bow.

DANCLA, Op. 74

Developing Finger Flexibility

Finger flexibility is a requisite in trill playing. It will not develop with its own accord, but rather must be acquired through certain routine practice procedures. The exercises given below, which were devised by the famous Polish violinist, Henri Wieniawski, will aid materially in developing this dexterity. However, these exercises must be practiced at a slow tempo, with the finger producing the upper tone in each instance raised in a deliberate manner and returned accurately to the fingerboard. Fingers not actively engaged in producing the tones indicated must be held down at all times.

BASIC STUDIES

WIENIAWSKI

Also practice similar exercises on the G String and the A String.

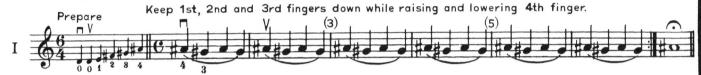

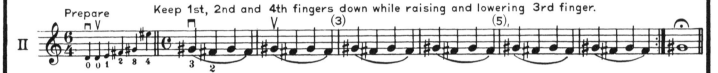

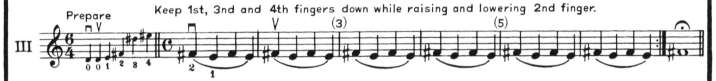

VARIANTS ON BASIC STUDIES

WIENIAWSKI

Also practice similar exercises on the G String and the A String.

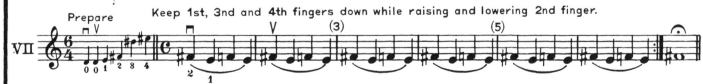

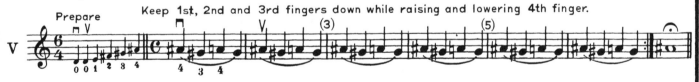

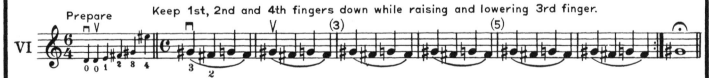

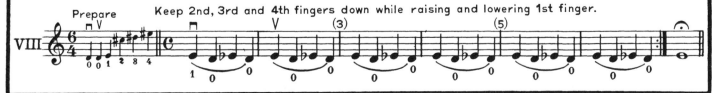

Trill Playing

WHISTLER

BASIC STUDIES

Practice similar exercises on the A, D & G strings.

PREPARATORY STUDIES

Play each 32nd note with as much rapidity as possible, the trill finger rebounding with elasticity and speed. Gradually increase tempo until each exercise becomes a trill. It does not matter how many notes a trill contains; the greater the number of notes, the better the trill will sound. Repeat each line many times.

Practice similar exercises on the A, D & G strings.

Trill Etudes

Trill Etude in C
(Whole Note and Half-Note Trills)

WOHLFAHRT, Op. 45

Play as many notes as possible in each trill. Raise trill finger with rapid light action.

Also practice each trill starting with the principal note, disregarding the acciaccatura.

Trill Etude in F
(Quarter-Note Trills)

WEISS, Op. 80

Play as many notes as possible in each trill. Raise trill finger with *rapid, light* action.

Also practice each trill starting with the principal note, disregarding the acciaccatura.

Trill Etude in B♭

WEISS, Op. 80

Play as many notes as possible in each trill. Raise trill finger with rapid, light action.

Trill Etude No. 1 in E♭

KAYSER, Op. 20

Play as many notes as possible in each trill. Raise trill finger with rapid, light action.

Trill Etude No. 2 in E♭

MAZAS, Op. 36

Play as many notes as possible in each trill. Raise trill finger with rapid, light action.

Double-Stop Playing

ALARD, Op. 10

> If difficulty is encountered in playing the studies of this page, the performer should turn at once to the comprehensive work, DEVELOPING DOUBLE-STOPS, by Harvey S. Whistler, and begin a thorough study of this phase of violin technic.

Equal pressure should be exerted by each finger when playing two tones simultaneously. Likewise, equal bow pressure should be used for each tone.

THIRDS

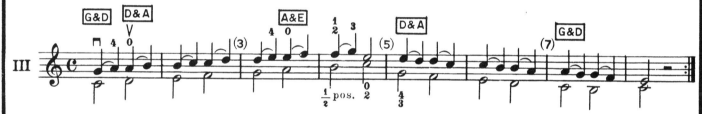

FOURTHS

FIFTHS

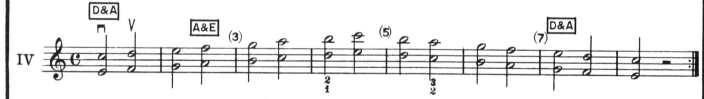

SIXTHS

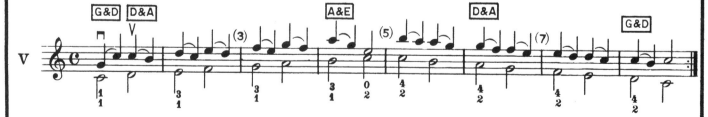

SEVENTHS

OCTAVES

Etudes In Double-Stops

Double-Stop Etude No.1 in G

DE BERIOT, Op. 102

To be played in legato style. Care should be taken to see that equal finger and bow pressures are used when producing each tone of the intervals.

Double-Stop Etude No. 2 in G

ALARD, Op. 10

To be played in legato style. Care should be taken to see that equal finger and bow pressures are used
when producing each tone of the intervals.

Double-Stop Etude No. 3 in G

WOHLFAHRT, Op. 74

To be played in legato style. Care should be taken to see that equal finger and bow pressures are used when producing each tone of the intervals.

Double-Stop Etude in D

ALARD, Op. 10

The accompaniment figuration, indicated by the lower notes, should be brought out in a distinct manner, while the melody is sustained as much as possible.

Double-Stop Etude in A

SITT, Op. 32

Also practice using a separate bow for each interval. Care should be taken to see that equal finger and bow pressures are used when producing each tone of the intervals.

Double-Stop Etude in C

BLUMENSTENGEL, Op. 33

Transfering from down bow to up bow, and vice versa, should be carried out as smoothly as possible, and changes of fingering should not interfere with the smooth, legato style of execution.

Double-Stop Etude in F

BLUMENSTENGEL, Op. 33

Practice slowly and maintain a steady tempo throughout. Equal bow pressure should be applied to both parts.

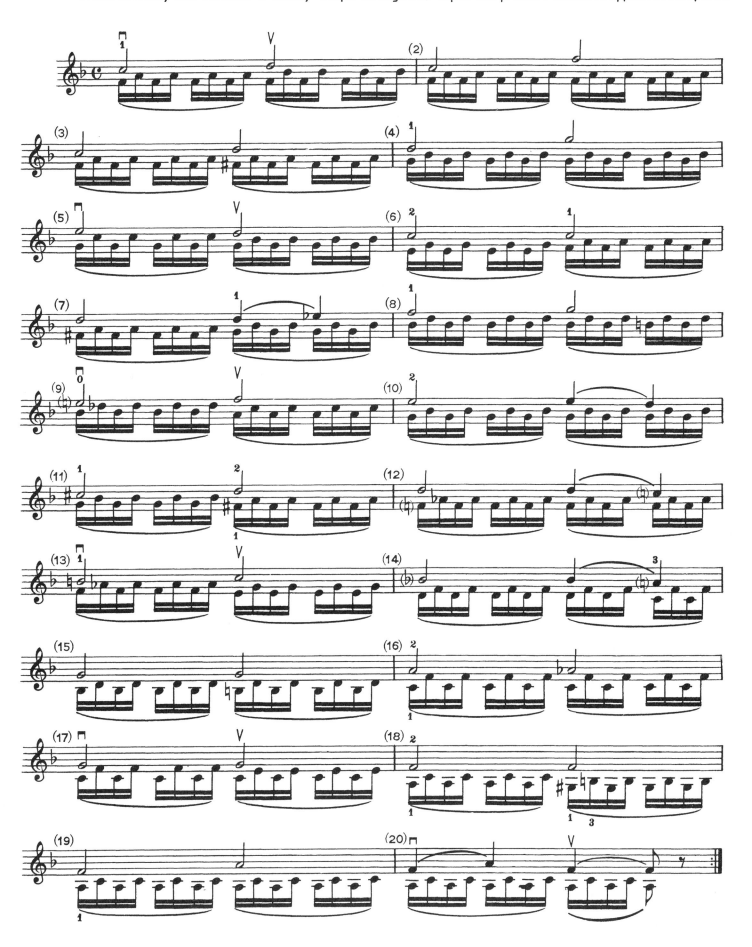

Double-Stop Etude in B♭

WOHLFAHRT, Op. 45

To be played in legato style. Care must be taken to see that equal finger and bow pressures are used when producing each tone of the intervals. Changes in fingering should not interfere with the over-all sustained effect.

Double-Stop Etude in E♭

LEONARD, Op. 21

To be played in a smooth, sustained manner. All double-stop shifting should be as inaudible as possible. Changes in fingering should not interfere with the over-all sustained effect.

Etude No. 1 in Prepared Octaves

BLUMENSTENGEL, Op. 33

Practice slowly. Listen carefully to both tones of the octave to be sure they are in tune with each other before playing them together. Keep 1st and 4th fingers permanently down unless other fingering is necessary.

Etude No. 1 in Octaves

BLUMENSTENGEL, Op. 33

Practice slowly. Do not proceed from one octave to the next until the intonation is correct.

Also practice sustaining each octave for (1) two counts, and (2) four counts.

Also practice (1) slurring each two octaves, and (2) slurring each complete measure.

Etude No. 2 in Prepared Octaves

KAYSER, Op. 20

Practice slowly. Listen carefully to both tones of the octave to be sure they are in tune with each other before playing them together. Keep 1st and 4th fingers permanently down unless other fingering is necessary.

Etude No. 2 in Octaves

KAYSER, Op. 20

Practice slowly. Do not proceed from one octave to the next until the intonation is correct.
Also practice sustaining each octave for (1) two counts, and (2) four counts.
Also practice (1) slurring each two octaves, and (2) slurring each complete measure.

Octave-Finale
(A Melodic Study)

WOHLFAHRT, Op. 54

Practice slowly. Do not proceed from one octave to the next until the intonation is correct.